Science@School | Book 5A

Keeping healthy

A brief history

TODAY... 1957 Albert Sabin develops a polio vaccine from live, weakened viruses... 1884 Max Rubner discovers that the body gets energy from carbohydrates and fats... 1884 Illich Mechnikov discovers how white blood cells destroy germs... 1879 Louis Pasteur discovers that bacteria can be weakened and used as a vaccine. He develops the theory of germs... 1875 Henry Clapp investigates the amount of vitamins and minerals needed for a healthy diet... 1804 Karl Rokitansky recognises bacteria as a cause of disease... 1796 Edward Jenner uses inoculation with cowpox to protect against smallpox in Britain... In 1775 the eating of limes is made compulsory on British ships, hence the nickname 'limey' for the British... 1775 William Withering uses digitalis, extracted from foxgloves, to treat heart disease... 1753 James Lind uses lemons containing vitamin C to cure scurvy... 1731 John Arbuthnot writes on how to cure some ailments by changing diet... 1701 Giacomo Pylarini inoculates children in Turkey with smallpox. This is probably the first inoculation anywhere... 1670 Thomas Willis shows a connection between sugar and diabetes... 1645 Daniel Whistler describes the disease rickets which is caused by a lack of vitamin D... 1626 Jan Baptista van Helmont suggests that diseases are caused by external agents that get into the body... 1530 Paracelsus is the first to use chemicals, not natural plants, as medicines... 170AD The Roman doctor Galen is the first to use the pulse to help understand illness... 130BC Asclepiades, in Turkey, believes that diseases are caused by a 'disturbance' to the 'particles' in the body... 400BC The Greek doctor Hippocrates writes the oath about keeping people healthy that every doctor is still bound by today.

For more information visit www.science-at-school.com

Dr Brian Knapp

Word list

These are some science words that you should look out for as you go through the book. They are shown using CAPITAL letters.

BACTERIUM
(plural BACTERIA)
An extremely tiny creature (microbe) that can live on or inside the body. It releases substances which can be poisonous and cause disease.

BALANCED DIET
A diet that keeps you healthy by giving the body the right proportions of what it needs.

BLOOD PRESSURE
The pressure of the blood in the blood vessels. If blood pressure is too high it can cause heart problems.

CALORIE
A measure of the energy in food. Units used are Calories (Cal) or kilocalories (kcal). You may find this on some food labels.

CARBOHYDRATE
An important energy-giving part of some food. There are two kinds of carbohydrate: starch and sugar.

CELLS
Tiny building blocks of the body. Cells are less than a tenth of a millimetre across. A cell is composed of a thin skin called a membrane, and contains a jelly-like substance and a darker structure called a nucleus.

CHOLESTEROL
A waxy, fat-like substance that is important in the blood. However, too much cholesterol can cause some of it to settle out and stick to blood vessels, causing heart attacks.

DIARRHOEA
Unusually fast passage of partly digested food through the gut. The result is frequent visits to the toilet.

DIET
The food that you normally eat. (Not a special kind of food.)

DISEASE
A change in some of the body's organs as a result of an attack by a microbe from outside (an infectious disease) or because of some change that occurs within the body (for example, cancer).

ENERGY
The power in food. It is locked away as chemicals, but released when we eat the food.

FAT
A substance found in food that provides a concentrated form of energy. It can come from animals or plants.

FOOD POISONING
A form of disease caused by certain bacteria in food you have eaten.

FOOD PYRAMID
A picture, shaped like a pyramid, which is designed to show the different amounts of food we can eat for a healthy diet.

MEDICINE
A drug that is designed to make you healthy.

MICROBE
A creature too small to be seen except with a powerful microscope.

MINERAL
A substance such as calcium or iron that is needed by the body.

PROTEIN
A substance found in food that your body uses to build new tissues.

STARCH
One of two kinds of carbohydrate. Starch is a high energy food. It is found in cereals, bread, pasta and potatoes.

VACCINE
A substance that is injected into a healthy person to help them produce their own body defences against a disease.

VIRUS
An extremely small kind of microbe.

VITAMINS
Special substances, such as vitamin C, that help the body to work well.

2

Contents

Weblink: www.science-at-school.com

Food and drink

Food and drink are essential if we are to stay alive.

Being healthy means being active and able to do all of the things you want to do. It means being able to resist disease and injury and expecting a long life.

Food and drink provide the **ENERGY** and nourishment for living. Each food contains its own unique combination of nourishment and energy. So healthy food is important for keeping a healthy body.

Water is a combination of oxygen and hydrogen. Our bodies are 80% water.

Other elements combine to make the rest of our body tissues and fluids.

Food variety

There are many kinds of food and drink, but every one is made of some, or all, of five groups of nutrients (Picture 1). They are called **CARBOHYDRATES** (sugar and **STARCH**), **FATS**, **PROTEINS**, **VITAMINS** and **MINERALS**.

Carbohydrates and fats give energy. Proteins are used to build new cells and repair old ones. Vitamins and minerals help build parts of the body like hair, teeth and bones, and keep us healthy. Because each type of food does a different job, the body needs food containing each group – you cannot just eat one type of food or do without water and stay healthy (Picture 2).

▲ **(Picture 1) Why you need to eat a variety of foods. Your body is the world's most complicated chemistry set. It contains these chemicals by percentage weight, along with 20 more chemicals in smaller amounts:**

Oxygen	65
Carbon	18
Hydrogen	10
Nitrogen	3
Calcium	2
Phosphorus	1.1
Sulphur	0.25
Potassium	0.20
Sodium	0.15
Chlorine	0.15
Magnesium	0.05
Iron	0.004
Copper	0.00015
Manganese	0.00013
Iodine	0.00004

All of these chemicals come from the food we eat. No one food contains all of these chemicals. We must eat a range of foods to make sure we get all of the chemicals we need. Most of these chemicals can be combined into one of five groups. We call the groups carbohydrates, fats, proteins, vitamins and minerals.

4

Sugars and starches

Natural sugars dissolve easily in water and are quickly used by the body. They are found in the largest amounts in fruit. The kind of sugar we use to sweeten food is not a natural sugar.

Starches provide energy to the body much more slowly. Starches are found in plant seeds, such as wheat, rice and maize, and in tubers such as potatoes.

Fat

The most concentrated form of energy is fat, a substance that makes up a large proportion of butter, cheese, milk and some kinds of meat and fish.

Fats are used as a reserve of energy. The body stores fat for use later. Most fat is stored just under the skin, where it also helps to slow down heat loss.

Proteins

Proteins are used in making and repairing the body. The main foods which contain proteins are meat, fish, eggs, milk, peas, beans and cereals.

Vitamins and minerals

Your body needs small amounts of many other substances, grouped together as vitamins and minerals. Vitamins serve many vital purposes, including helping to break down our food and fighting disease. Minerals include calcium for building bones and teeth (Picture 3), sodium and potassium, which are used in every part of your body.

▼ (Picture 2) Our bodies are mostly water, so water is an important part of our diet.

Water on its own is good for us, but it also contains many invisible minerals and other chemicals that are good for our bodies too.

▶ (Picture 3) Some drinks, like milk, have high concentrations of minerals, fat and sugar and are as much food as drink.

Milk contains many useful minerals such as calcium. It also has lots of vitamin D.

Summary
- The body needs food and drink for energy and to build up and repair the body.
- No single food contains all the things we need.
- The body needs water in addition to food.

Weblink: www.science-at-school.com

Too few vitamins and too little fibre

The body needs a range of materials to remain healthy. However, if some vital ingredient is missing, poor health and even death can result.

Some of the most vital substances for healthy living are needed in only tiny amounts. These substances are vitamins. Here are just two examples of what happens when one of these vitamins is in short supply.

Lack of vitamin D

Vitamin D is carried through the blood and helps control the level of calcium in bones.

When vitamin D is in short supply, there is nothing to instruct the body to keep sending calcium to the bones. As a result, bones become soft. Leg bones, for example, do not harden properly and sometimes bend under the weight of the body, giving bow legs. This disease is called rickets.

The body can make vitamin D from sunlight, but fish oils can also supply vitamin D (Picture 1). As a result, fish oils were prescribed as early as the 18th century. However, it was only

▼ (Picture 1) Fish oils, milk and other dairy products are a good source of vitamin D. Other foods that contain lots of vitamin D are liver, eggs and cereals.

after experiments on animals in 1918 that the vital ingredient in fish oil was found to be vitamin D. Milk is now also known to be a source of vitamin D, and in many countries milk is enriched with extra vitamin D by law.

Lack of vitamin C

People who have a lack of vitamin C get a disease called scurvy in which the body slowly falls apart. The first signs are bleeding gums and loose teeth, but in severe cases people die.

The reason for this is that vitamin C (Picture 2) is vital in making sure the tissues that hold the body together remain healthy.

The relationship between scurvy and vitamin C was an early medical success. In 1753, Scottish naval surgeon James

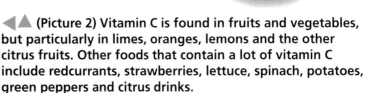

(Picture 2) Vitamin C is found in fruits and vegetables, but particularly in limes, oranges, lemons and the other citrus fruits. Other foods that contain a lot of vitamin C include redcurrants, strawberries, lettuce, spinach, potatoes, green peppers and citrus drinks.

Lind showed that scurvy could be cured and prevented by eating fresh oranges, lemons or limes. Eating citrus fruit became compulsory on all British ships. When other sailors saw the British eating limes they gave them the nickname of limeys.

Fibre

Fibre, or roughage, is the part of a plant that we cannot digest (Pictures 3 and 4). It keeps the other food we haven't digested bulky and moist so that it can be easily carried through our gut. This flushes out poisonous substances and reduces the chance of diseases developing in the lower part of our digestive system.

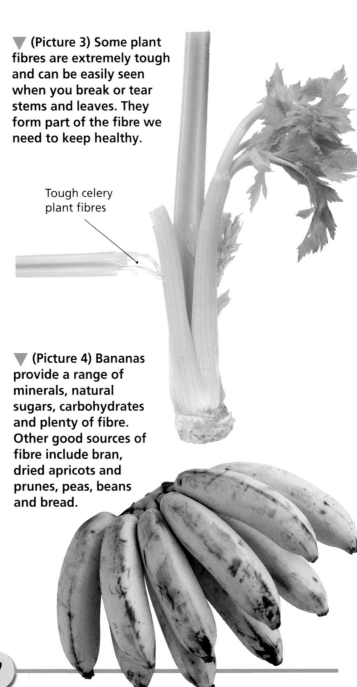

(Picture 3) Some plant fibres are extremely tough and can be easily seen when you break or tear stems and leaves. They form part of the fibre we need to keep healthy.

Tough celery plant fibres

(Picture 4) Bananas provide a range of minerals, natural sugars, carbohydrates and plenty of fibre. Other good sources of fibre include bran, dried apricots and prunes, peas, beans and bread.

Summary

- Vitamins are needed for helping the body work well.
- Fibre is needed to carry waste materials through our bodies.
- We can be healthy only if we have enough vitamins and fibre in our diets.

Too much fat and salt

The body will make use of what it is given. But if it is given too much of some food, ill health can result.

As with all animals, human bodies have a built-in ability to make the most of what is available – to protect the body against times when there is not enough. This is why the body stores up essential materials that give us energy.

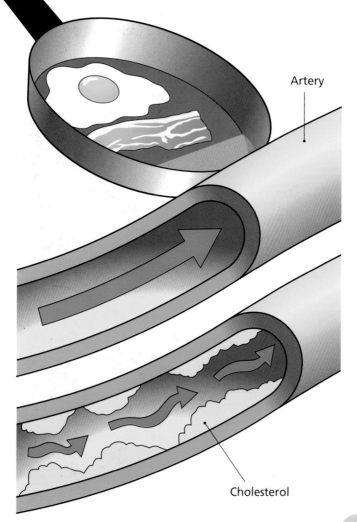

▼ (Picture 1) Animal foods like bacon and egg contain cholesterol. If there is too much cholesterol in the blood it may settle out on the artery walls. This obstructs the flow of blood and may lead to blood clots and even heart attacks.

Artery

Cholesterol

Too much fat

If we cannot immediately make use of all of the energy in the food we eat, our bodies begin to store it away in the most concentrated and efficient form possible – as fat.

Cholesterol

CHOLESTEROL is a waxy, fat-like substance which is made in the liver and carried around in the blood. It is vital in small amounts. All animals make cholesterol, and it is concentrated in their fat. So, when we eat animal fat we also take in extra cholesterol – sometimes more than the body needs.

Sometimes, if the level of cholesterol is too high, some of the surplus cholesterol settles out and sticks to the walls of the blood vessels, leaving less room for the blood to flow (Picture 1). This is the main cause of heart disease.

When the arteries are narrowed, the heart has to push with greater force (one of the causes of high BLOOD PRESSURE). In some cases, the waxy coating may break up and pieces may block the blood vessels, stopping the flow of blood. The result may be a heart attack. If the blood supply to the brain is blocked, it is called a stroke.

Salt

Salt (Pictures 2 and 3) is a mineral found in many foods. It is extremely important for the proper working of muscles, and for getting nourishment into the blood. You would die without salt, but too much salt can also lead to high blood pressure and heart disease.

Preventing heart disease

The threat of heart disease can be lessened by exercise. This helps the body use up more cholesterol. Eating a balanced **DIET** that does not contain too much animal fat or salt can also reduce the chance of heart disease. (However, the most important way of reducing the risk of heart disease is not to smoke.)

There are lots of easy ways to eat less animal fats, for example, by eating only the lean parts of meat, not the fatty parts, keeping down the amount of cream, butter and cheese you eat, and draining off the fat after cooking instead of adding it to gravy.

It is not necessary to cut out all animal fats or salt to stay healthy, just to keep the amount down.

◀ (Picture 2) The Romans knew how vital salt was. A lot of salt is lost through sweat, when we are hot or doing hard work. Roman soldiers worked hard and would get very tired or ill without extra salt. So instead of money they were often paid in salt – or *salarium* as they called it. *Salarium* is the origin of the word salary we use today. Many of us are not as active as Roman soldiers would have been and so we need less salt.

◀▼ (Picture 3) Salt is a very good and cheap preservative and so it is used in food that needs to keep for a while. However, fast food, such as a small pre-prepared pizza, may contain more than an entire day's supply of salt. Sauces also contain a lot of salt (see page 13).

Summary

- Heart disease is often caused by increased blood pressure.
- Too much cholesterol and salt can cause high blood pressure.
- Eating sensibly can keep blood pressure under control.

Do you eat a balanced diet?

A balanced diet means eating a suitable amount of each of the main food groups.

Your body needs a certain amount of nourishment and energy if it is to stay healthy. How much you need depends on how active you are, but the proportions of each type of food you eat should be generally the same.

A normal diet

The food that you normally eat over a period of time such as a day, week or year is called your **DIET**. Your body will only be healthy if it gets the right balance of carbohydrates, vitamins and minerals, proteins and fat (Picture 1). This is called a **BALANCED DIET**. But how do we know what 'enough' means, and how can we tell if our diet is balanced?

Weight

First, it helps to know that the body is very good at looking after itself. It also helps to know that the body likes to have

Fats: vegetable oils, margarine, nuts, butter, fatty meat, cream, cheese.

Proteins: eggs, meat, fish, nuts, lentils, peas, beans and dairy products.

Vitamins and minerals: fruit, vegetables, liver, milk.

Carbohydrates (starch and natural sugars): cereals, bread, pasta, rice, potatoes, beans.

▲ (Picture 1) This is a FOOD PYRAMID. It shows the proportions of various foods you need if you want to eat a balanced and healthy diet. You should eat a larger amount of those foods at the bottom of the pyramid and only small amounts of those at the top.

plenty of insurance, so if it can store food in case of emergencies, it will. The difficulty is that the more it stores, the heavier the body becomes and the harder other parts of the body have to work.

A healthy diet for fully grown people is, in part, one where the body does not gain or lose weight. We can find this out by knowing how much energy is in

Weblink: www.science-at-school.com

our food (which is measured in a unit called **CALORIES**) and how much energy we burn off by living (which we can also measure in Calories).

Younger people are growing and getting heavier all the time. For them, increasing weight is often normal, but getting lighter is not.

Daily needs

A simple rule for eating a balanced diet is to eat one portion of meat and one portion of dairy products a day, and one or more portions of each of the other groups, such as fruit, as shown in Picture 2. You should aim to eat five portions of fruits and vegetables each day – this is the ideal to aim for.

A rule for how much to eat is not to eat more calories than your body needs.

Summary
- To follow a balanced diet, use the food pyramid.
- Try to avoid sugary and fatty foods.
- Eat lots of foods containing starch, fibre, protein, vitamins and minerals.

Morning meal

Cereal and milk

Orange juice

◀▼ (Picture 2) There are many different ways to get a balanced diet. Some people choose not to eat meat, or eat only certain types of meat, and others choose food from different cultures. Some people have a larger morning meal and a smaller evening meal. Some people eat several small meals. But whatever way you eat your food, you should have roughly the right proportions of each type of food from the food pyramid, and roughly the same calories to get a balanced diet. This diagram gives you an example.

Midday meal

Sandwich with cheese, lettuce and tomato filling (uncooked vegetables contain more vitamins and minerals).

Milk

Banana

Fruit salad

Vegetables such as potatoes, peas and carrots.

Water

Evening meal

Meat such as chicken and lamb.

Weblink: www.science-at-school.com

A lunch to think about

To see whether your diet is balanced, you have to know your weight, and what is in each food.

Confused about how much to eat? You can get a rough guide to your diet needs easily by following these steps.

Your diet needs

A rough guide to your energy needs – in Calories (Cal) – will be your weight in kilograms (kg) multiplied by 32. If, for example, you weigh 45kg and do an average amount of exercise*, then your body will burn up $45 \times 32 = 1{,}440$ Calories each day.

Carbohydrates

You should get about six-tenths of your diet needs from carbohydrates each day. This is $1{,}440 \times {}^{6}/_{10} = 864$ Calories.

There are about 4 Calories in every gram (g) weight of carbohydrate, so you can eat $864 \div 4 = 216$g of carbohydrate a day.

Fat

You should get no more than three-tenths of your energy from fat. This is half as much as carbohydrates = 432 Calories. As there are 9 Calories in each gram of

fat (fat is a more concentrated source of energy), you should eat no more than $432 \div 9 = 48$g of fat.

Fibre

You need to eat 20 to 30g of fibre a day from plant sources (animal foods do not contain fibre). You can include peanuts and raw vegetables such as celery and carrots in this.

Sodium

You should keep your sodium (salt) level below 2,400 milligrams (mg) a day. This is about a teaspoon of salt. Most processed and convenience foods contain large amounts of salt.

Cholesterol

You want to keep your cholesterol below 300mg a day.

▼ (Picture 1) Janet and Jack's lunch.

* Note: If you do not exercise regularly, then instead of multiplying your weight by 32, multiply it by 28; if you are a sporting type multiply by 36.

Weblink: www.science-at-school.com

Janet and Jack's lunch

Janet and Jack, who each weigh 45kg, both have a big hamburger, a medium portion of French fries, a glass of cola and a portion of sauce for lunch (Picture 1).

The table below (Picture 2) shows you what their food contained. As you can see, in just this lunch Janet and Jack have eaten nearly all of their day's energy, nearly twice as much fat and more than the salt they need in a whole day. But they have eaten only two-thirds of the carbohydrate and a quarter of the fibre they need.

Diet turned upside down

In this meal Janet and Jack have turned the food pyramid (Page 10) upside down (Picture 3). To have a balanced diet they would now need to eat nothing but low energy, high fibre food, such as fruit, for one of their other meals.

Summary
- Unless you are growing fast, what you eat should balance what you burn as energy.
- Most processed and fast foods contain lots of fat and sodium.
- The best source of energy is from starchy foods, not fatty ones.

▼ (Picture 2) This table shows the contents of Janet and Jack's lunch.

Food	Quantity	Calories	Fat (g)	Cholesterol (mg)	Sodium (mg)	Carbohydrates (g)	Fibre (g)
Cola	One glass	140	0	0	50	39	0
Hamburger	200g	600	40	125	1,000	28	1
French fries	medium 120g	400	21	0	1,240	86	6
Sauce	30g portion	170	17	0	200	2	0
TOTAL		1,310	78	125	2,490	155	7
Recommended for one day		1,440	48	300	2,400	216	30

▼ (Picture 3) This is a food pyramid turned upside down by Janet and Jack.

Recommended for one day 100%

Fat 143%

Sodium 104%

Calories 91%

Carbohydrate 71%

Cholesterol 42%

Fibre 23%

13

Why exercise?

By moving about, getting slightly warm and getting a red face, you help your heart, lungs, muscles and bones.

If you walk, jog, cycle, swim, play a sport or do any kind of exercise that keeps you moving fairly quickly for some time, you will feel slightly warm, go red in the face and begin to sweat

▼ (Picture 1) Exercise doesn't need to involve running a marathon. Regular fast walking, such as walking about 3km a day, or playing a game in the playground, is all you may need. Exercise gets your muscles working, helps your blood circulation and reduces the excess fat in your body. It also makes your bones stronger and heavier.

gently. This is enough to keep the body healthy (Picture 1). Here is why.

Bone health

Bones are just as alive as any other part of the body. They are continually growing and changing. When you move about for a while, you jolt the bones and this makes them become more dense and strong. Lack of moderate exercise causes bones to do the reverse, becoming less dense and weaker and more liable to break.

Heart and muscle health

When you exercise you make your muscles work harder. More blood vessels will grow to supply the larger muscles. Hard-working muscles are stronger and more able to cope with any sudden need for movement.

The heart is a muscle and, like all muscles, it works better when it is exercised (Pictures 2 and 3). A healthy person cannot damage their heart by working it hard. They can only strengthen it.

Red face meter

When your body changes food into energy it releases the extra energy it can't use as heat. To get rid of the heat, your

Weblink: www.science-at-school.com

▼ (Picture 2) Pulse and the body.
The heart pumps the blood around the body. The heart is connected to the tubes (blood vessels) that carry fresh blood (red) from the heart, and return used blood (blue) back to the heart.

Each time your heart works, it sends a wave, or pulse, of high pressure blood through your body. You can feel this pulse most easily in the big blood vessels (arteries) that run close to the surface of the skin. The main pulse points are shown as pink dots.

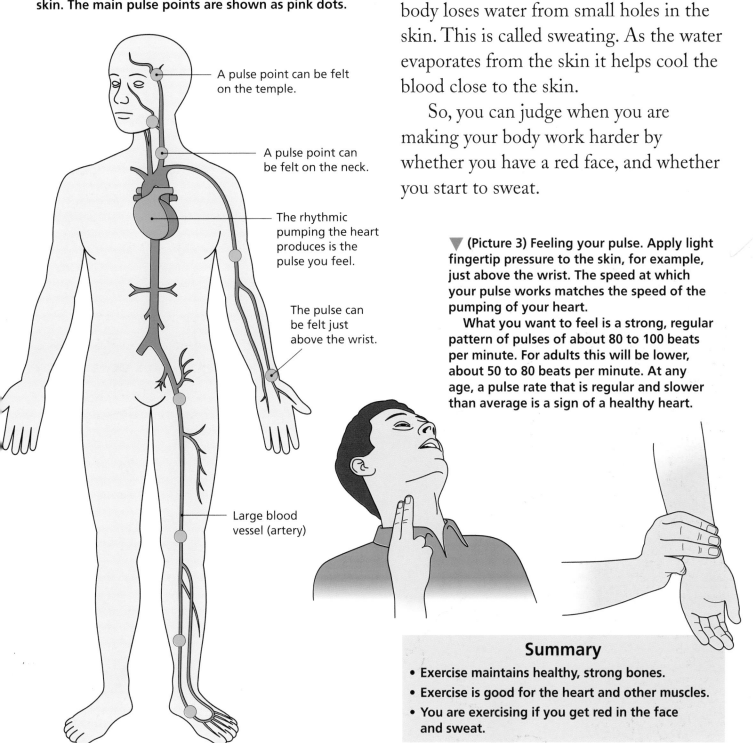

A pulse point can be felt on the temple.

A pulse point can be felt on the neck.

The rhythmic pumping the heart produces is the pulse you feel.

The pulse can be felt just above the wrist.

Large blood vessel (artery)

body sends more blood to blood vessels close to the skin, so that extra heat can be released into the surrounding air. In young people, you see the extra blood as a red face.

To help you lose even more heat, your body loses water from small holes in the skin. This is called sweating. As the water evaporates from the skin it helps cool the blood close to the skin.

So, you can judge when you are making your body work harder by whether you have a red face, and whether you start to sweat.

▼ (Picture 3) Feeling your pulse. Apply light fingertip pressure to the skin, for example, just above the wrist. The speed at which your pulse works matches the speed of the pumping of your heart.

What you want to feel is a strong, regular pattern of pulses of about 80 to 100 beats per minute. For adults this will be lower, about 50 to 80 beats per minute. At any age, a pulse rate that is regular and slower than average is a sign of a healthy heart.

Summary
- Exercise maintains healthy, strong bones.
- Exercise is good for the heart and other muscles.
- You are exercising if you get red in the face and sweat.

Weblink: www.science-at-school.com

Recovering from disease

A DISEASE is an illness brought on by something going wrong with the cells in the body.

Our bodies are made of trillions of tiny building blocks called **CELLS**. The body works in such a delicate balance that even a few cells working wrongly can cause severe health problems.

Infectious diseases

Infectious diseases are the most common illnesses. They occur when tiny creatures called **MICROBES** (mainly **BACTERIA** and **VIRUSES**) destroy cells. Disease-causing microbes are known as germs, and the illness you get from them is called an infectious disease.

Infectious diseases are carried between one person and another in the air, in water or by touch (Picture 1). For example, germs are spread when someone sneezes, or in food that has not been cooked properly or on crockery and cutlery that has not been washed thoroughly.

Because your hands are frequently touching things that other people have handled, infection can enter the body when you put your fingers into your mouth or rub your eyes. This is particularly the case when people visit the toilet and then do not wash their hands properly.

Bacteria are the main cause of diseases such as **FOOD POISONING** (Picture 2) and tuberculosis. The common cold and influenza are examples of diseases produced by viruses.

How the body copes with disease

The body has its own defences to cope with infectious diseases. Since most bacteria can only live within a small range of temperatures, the body often fights bacteria by developing a fever, sending the temperature far above that at which bacteria can thrive. Special cells called white blood cells also travel through the blood looking for bacteria. They then capture the bacteria and destroy it (Picture 3). Doctors can also help with

▼ **(Picture 1) Harmful bacteria and other germs can be spread as people touch objects such as handles and doors.**

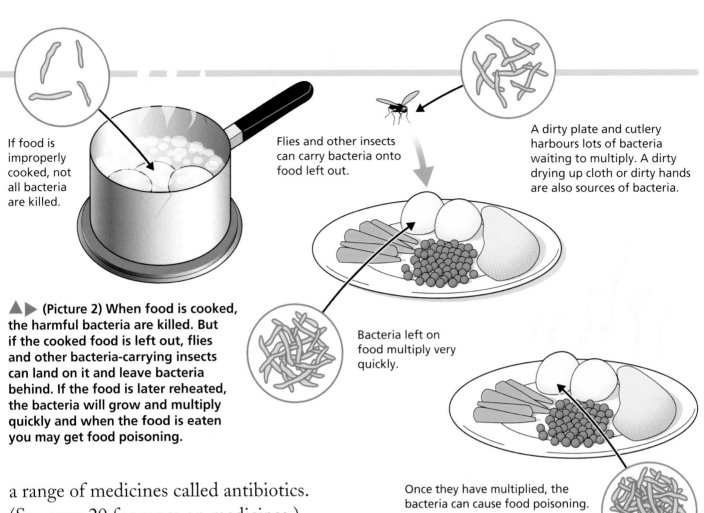

If food is improperly cooked, not all bacteria are killed.

Flies and other insects can carry bacteria onto food left out.

A dirty plate and cutlery harbours lots of bacteria waiting to multiply. A dirty drying up cloth or dirty hands are also sources of bacteria.

▲▶ (Picture 2) When food is cooked, the harmful bacteria are killed. But if the cooked food is left out, flies and other bacteria-carrying insects can land on it and leave bacteria behind. If the food is later reheated, the bacteria will grow and multiply quickly and when the food is eaten you may get food poisoning.

Bacteria left on food multiply very quickly.

Once they have multiplied, the bacteria can cause food poisoning.

a range of medicines called antibiotics. (See page 20 for more on medicines.)

Viruses are much more difficult for the body to cope with because a virus is very tiny, and it burrows its way inside healthy cells. Very often, in a virus attack, the infection simply has to be allowed to take its course.

The most effective way to stop many virus infections is by using a **VACCINE**, which is a weakened form of the virus. The body can more easily overwhelm the weakened form and can build up the resistance to fight off a future attack by the full-strength virus.

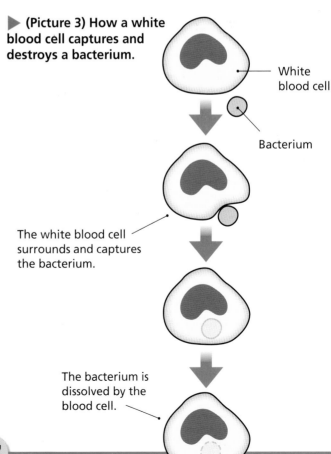

▶ (Picture 3) How a white blood cell captures and destroys a bacterium.

White blood cell

Bacterium

The white blood cell surrounds and captures the bacterium.

The bacterium is dissolved by the blood cell.

Summary
- **Diseases are illnesses caused by germs, often bacteria or viruses.**
- **Bacteria can be killed by white cells in the body, and by antibiotics.**
- **Viruses are often prepared for by using a vaccine.**

Coping with injury

An injury occurs when something damages, bruises, cuts, crushes or breaks part of the body.

Accidents do happen. You may drop a hammer on your foot, cut yourself on a piece of broken glass or you may be involved in a sports or car accident. Doctors call a sudden injury a trauma.

How the body copes with injury

When you are injured, some body cells are destroyed and others are damaged. It will take time for new cells to be produced. Some types of wound, such as open wounds, are also open to attack from germs in the air (Picture 1). The body therefore has to have a way of making sure the injury does not get worse (it must be stabilised), so it has to begin to repair and it has to ward off disease that can enter an open wound.

Stages of recovery

The main features of an injury are redness, heat, swelling and pain.

If you are injured, blood vessels immediately enlarge near to the injury and more blood than normal flows into the injured area. Chemicals are also

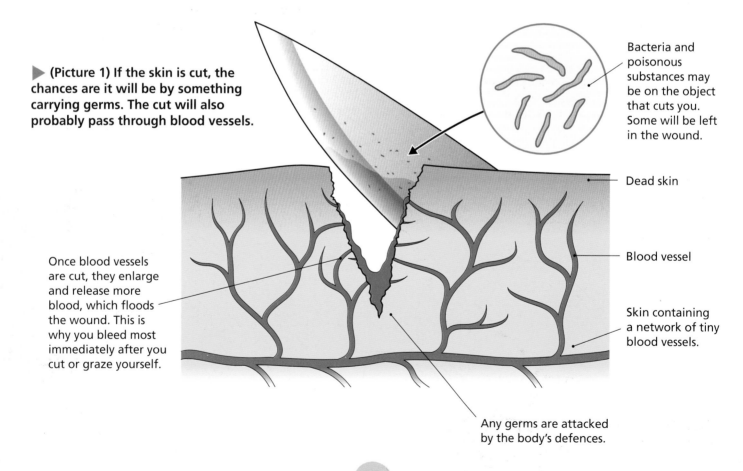

▶ (Picture 1) If the skin is cut, the chances are it will be by something carrying germs. The cut will also probably pass through blood vessels.

Bacteria and poisonous substances may be on the object that cuts you. Some will be left in the wound.

Dead skin

Blood vessel

Skin containing a network of tiny blood vessels.

Once blood vessels are cut, they enlarge and release more blood, which floods the wound. This is why you bleed most immediately after you cut or graze yourself.

Any germs are attacked by the body's defences.

Weblink: www.science-at-school.com

released that encourage blood flow. All of this is to wash any infection out of the injured area. White cells in the blood quickly set about killing bacteria. The extra blood flowing in the blood vessels makes the area near the injury look red, while the enlarged blood vessels and extra white cells cause swelling.

Once the blood has started to flow out, new substances in the blood – called platelets – are made. These reach the injury and begin to build up in the wound, sealing it off. That is why blood stops flowing from injuries after a while. The platelets form blood clots which stick in the blood vessels and act like a plug.

Heat in the area of the injury is also caused by the increased blood flow. At the same time, nerves near the wound send signals to your brain, which you feel as pain, reminding you that you have an injury to deal with quickly.

In time, new cells grow and repair the damaged area.

Medical help

Small injuries can be dealt with by the body without any more help than sticking plaster, but large injuries may need the help of doctors. Often, doctors will stitch the wound closed to give the body the chance to seal the wound more easily and with less chance of infection.

Summary
• An injury will cause redness, heat, swelling and pain.
• The body copes with an injury by washing it out with blood and attacking any germs.
• Large injuries often need the help of a doctor.

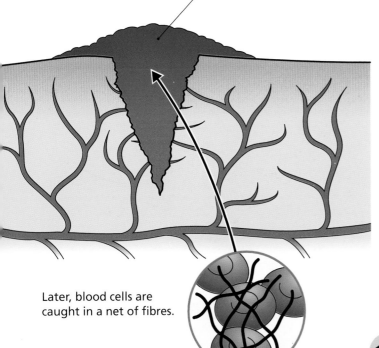

After a while platelets arrive at the wound and build up, forming a clot (scab) and sealing off the gap.

Later, blood cells are caught in a net of fibres.

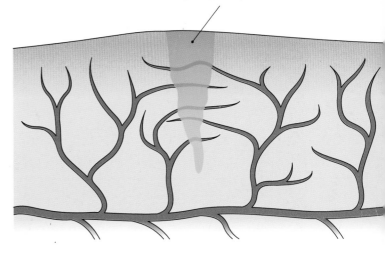

Cells grow to replace the damaged tissue. A scar may be left and seen as shiny skin on the surface.

Weblink: www.science-at-school.com

Medicines (medical drugs)

Medicines are substances taken to relieve pain or fight disease. They are designed to make a patient well again.

The word drug is a general term for any chemical that affects the way the body works. Drugs designed to make the body well are called **MEDICINES**.

Long ago, people discovered that substances in some plants helped to cure illness. These 'natural' cures included the pain-killer aspirin (which came from a material extracted from a willow tree) and the drug to help heart-attack sufferers called digitalis (which comes from the foxglove).

How drugs work

Today we have a much clearer understanding of how drugs work. This has allowed chemists to make a wide range of drugs that can treat more ailments than the natural cures could.

Drugs do one of two things: they balance materials that the body lacks or has too much of, or they change the way cells work.

Replacing chemicals

There are different kinds of substances in the body that drugs help to replace, or keep in balance. Some illnesses are due to lack of vitamins (see pages 6 and 7). Other illnesses occur when the body fails to produce important substances

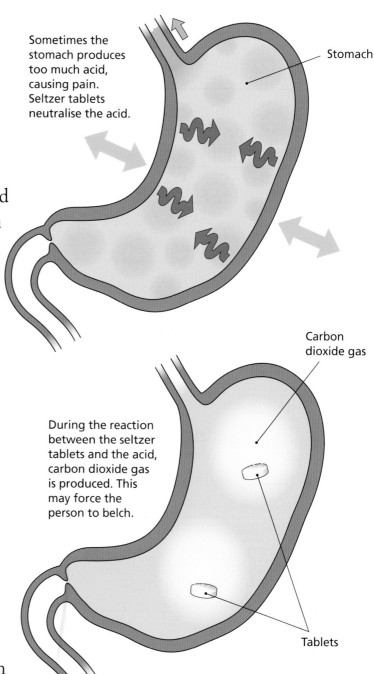

Sometimes the stomach produces too much acid, causing pain. Seltzer tablets neutralise the acid.

Stomach

Carbon dioxide gas

During the reaction between the seltzer tablets and the acid, carbon dioxide gas is produced. This may force the person to belch.

Tablets

▲ (Picture 1) The stomach churns food and mixes it with acids and other substances. Sometimes too much acid collects, causing stomach ache, indigestion or 'heart burn'.

Seltzer tablets (which are made of a substance that reacts with acid and neutralises it) are used to stop these forms of stomach ache.

Weblink: www.science-at-school.com

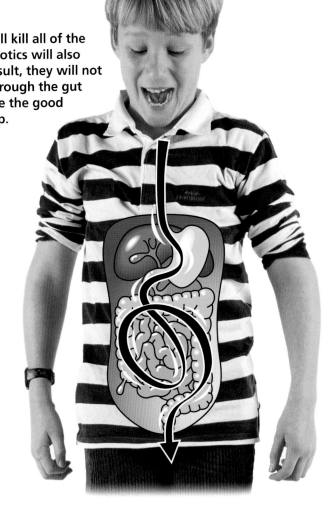

▶ **(Picture 2)** When antibiotics are taken, the drug will kill all of the bad bacteria, making you well again. However, antibiotics will also kill most of the good bacteria lining your gut. As a result, they will not be able to help absorb food and the food will pass through the gut quickly, causing DIARRHOEA. This is the side effect. Once the good bacteria have multiplied again, the diarrhoea will stop.

called hormones – such as insulin, which prevents diabetes. Sometimes, the body makes too much of a substance, such as stomach acid. Balancing medicines, in this case seltzer tablets, can correct this (Picture 1).

Changing how cells work

Drugs can act on cells throughout the body. When the body becomes injured (for example by straining a muscle), the natural reaction of the body is to cause the injured area to swell up and become inflamed. This can be reduced by slowing down the natural processes, which also relieves pain. Other drugs can be used to make the body's defences speed up.

The other way drugs can be used is to destroy germs such as bacteria. Some drugs can seek out and destroy germs or stop the germs from multiplying and give the body's own defences time to kill them.

Side effects

Once drugs get into the body they will change all of the cells of a certain type. For example, a drug designed to reduce a digestive problem may also cause the mouth to become dry, and make it more difficult to go to the toilet.

These unwanted results (which occur with natural cures as well as chemical ones) are called side effects (Picture 2).

In general, all drugs have side effects, but usually they are small compared to the effect of making someone well. Doctors prescribe doses of medicines that will give the best results with the smallest side effects. This is why following the correct dosage exactly is so important.

Summary
- Medicines are drugs designed to help you to get well.
- One group of drugs replaces substances that the body lacks.
- Other groups of drugs help the cells in the body.

Weblink: www.science-at-school.com

What are harmful drugs?

All chemical substances that we take are drugs, whether solids, liquids or gases. The dangerous ones are those that can cause permanent harm.

The body is a very tolerant chemistry set. But there are limits to what it can take. When you go beyond these limits then things may start to go wrong. We might find ourselves taking risks with our bodies.

The effects of smoking

Some chemicals, such as those in tobacco smoke, affect our breathing. The chemicals can block the lungs from taking in oxygen, or they may stop dirt in the throat from being removed naturally. As a result, germs can reach the lungs (Picture 1).

If germs get to the lungs, the only way the body can destroy them is by using white cells in the blood. But this causes an irritation to the airways, called bronchitis. The body then attempts to clear the lungs by coughing.

▼ (Picture 1) Some of the harmful effects of smoking.

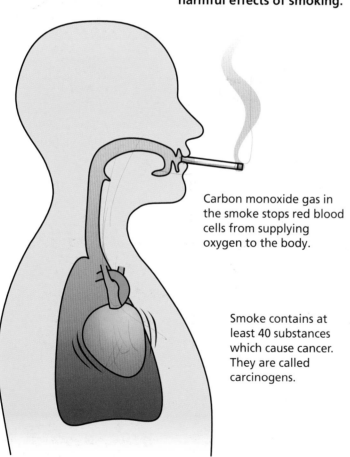

Carbon monoxide gas in the smoke stops red blood cells from supplying oxygen to the body.

Smoke contains at least 40 substances which cause cancer. They are called carcinogens.

The nicotine in cigarettes is an addictive drug. It raises the heart rate, causing a rushing sensation. The increased blood pressure puts a strain on the heart.

The tar in cigarette smoke can coat the airways and lungs, just as it coats this spoon. This makes the smoker much more prone to colds, bronchitis and lung disease.

Smoke not breathed in by the smoker can instead be breathed in by nearby people. This is called passive smoking and it can cause harm to non-smokers.

Smoke also clings to clothing and other materials, leaving a strong smell, and after a period of time it stains everything it touches.

Weblink: www.science-at-school.com

Drugs can alter the state of the mind, making the user see things that do not exist, become unnaturally active, have dulled senses or even become violent. People's reactions to drugs vary and are unpredictable.

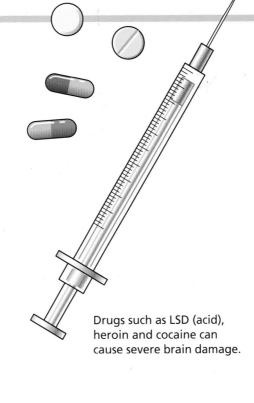

Drugs such as LSD (acid), heroin and cocaine can cause severe brain damage.

Chemicals such as solvents cause severe damage to the lungs and brain.

Alcohol is also an addictive drug and can destroy the liver and other organs if taken in large amounts on a regular basis.

▲ (Picture 2) Substance abuse is often addictive (habit-forming). Addicts stop taking care of themselves, so they exercise little, eat poorly and become prone to disease.

Coughing is a very violent activity, and if it is repeated over a long time it can damage lung tissue.

The chemicals in smoke may also affect the way some of the cells grow and make them develop abnormally. This is called cancer. In time, the cancer cells may spread through the body and may cause death.

Alcohol

Alcohol is a liquid found in beer, wine and spirits. In large amounts it can change behaviour. Taken over many years, it can cause liver failure and death.

Substance abuse

The chemicals in many solvents and illegal drugs affect the way the brain cells work. If solvents like glue are sniffed, or certain illegal drugs, such as ecstasy, are taken, then a change in behaviour may occur. Any substance taken in very large amounts can destroy brain cells or kill (Picture 2).

Summary
• Some substances can do the body far more harm than good.
• Tobacco and illegal drugs are harmful in any amount.
• Alcohol can be harmful if taken in excess.

Weblink: www.science-at-school.com

Index

Science@School

Science@School is a series published by Atlantic Europe Publishing Company Ltd.

 Atlantic Europe Publishing

Teacher's Guide
There is a Teacher's Guide to accompany this book, available only from the publisher.

CD-ROMs
There are browser-based CD-ROMs containing information to support the series. They are available from the publisher.

Dedicated Web Site
There's more information about other great Science@School packs and a wealth of supporting material available at our dedicated web site:

www.science-at-school.com

First published in 2002 by
Atlantic Europe Publishing Company Ltd

Copyright © 2002
Atlantic Europe Publishing Company Ltd

All rights reserved. No part of this publication may be reproduced, stored in a retrieval system, or transmitted in any form or by any means, electronic, mechanical, photocopying, recording or otherwise, without prior permission of the publisher.

Author
Brian Knapp, BSc, PhD

Educational Consultant
Peter Riley, BSc, C Biol, MI Biol, PGCE

Medical Consultant
Andrew Burnett, MB.ChB, MRCGP, DRCOG

Art Director
Duncan McCrae, BSc

Senior Designer
Adele Humphries, BA, PGCE

Editor
Lisa Magloff, BA

Illustrations
David Woodroffe

Designed and produced by
EARTHSCAPE EDITIONS

Reproduced in Malaysia by
Global Colour

Printed in Hong Kong by
Wing King Tong Company Ltd

Science@School
Volume 5A *Keeping healthy*
A CIP record for this book is available from the British Library.

Paperback ISBN 1 86214 148 7

Picture credits
All photographs are from the Earthscape Editions photolibrary.

This product is manufactured from sustainable managed forests. For every tree cut down at least one more is planted.